A Gift For

From

This edition published by The Greenwich Workshop, Inc.
exclusively for Hallmark Cards, Inc. For more information about
limited edition reproductions of Paul Landry's paintings, contact:
The Greenwich Workshop, Inc., PO Box 875, Shelton, CT 06484.

Design: Sheryl P. Kober
Editorial: Todd Hafer
ISBN: 0-86713-079-2

Printed in China

At The
Heart of Christmas

With the Art of Paul Landry

♔
Hallmark
GIFT BOOKS

BOK 6062

THE
HEART
OF
CHRISTMAS

When the last carol has been sung,
When the final gift has been unwrapped,
When the relatives have returned home,
When the lights and decorations have been put away…

Then the real work of Christmas begins:

To find the lost,
To heal the brokenhearted,
To feed the hungry,
To bring peace among enemies,
To rebuild what has been torn down,
To see the beauty all around,
To keep the holiday magic alive all year…

That is the true heart of Christmas.

There's majesty in every star,
in every snow-filled sky,
so take hold of every moment—
don't let Christmas pass you by.

*Christmas...
one word says it all.*

*Such magic is there in
Christmas to draw the
absent ones home.
Our hearts grow tender
with childhood memories
and love of kindred,
and we are better
having, in spirit, become
a child again at Christmas.*

—Laura Ingalls Wilder

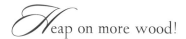eap on more wood!

The wind is chill;

But let it whistle

as it will,

We'll keep our Christmas

merry still.

—Sir Walter Scott

Winter's hush gives us time to pause...

and remember...

*Though years have passed
and now I have
traditions of my own,
The love that fills
my holidays,
is the love
I learned at home.*

—Vicki Kuyper

For somehow not only at Christmas,

But all the long year through,

The joy that you give to others

Is the joy that comes back to you.

And the more you spend in blessing

The poor and lonely and sad,

The more of your heart's possessing

Returns to make you glad.

— John Greenleaf Whittier

*To children who
spend Christmas
in a warm and
loving home,
heaven does not
seem like such
a faraway place.*

As winter approaches
we take heart in these things—
the green on the fir tree
and birds on the wing,
the hoped-for reunions,
a child's face all aglow,
the warmth of a fire,
the whisper of snow.

On every Christmas morning,
hope, faith, and wonder
are born again.

Memories of long ago…
Smiles beneath the mistletoe…
Cheeks aglow with winter's kiss…
'Tis the time to reminisce.

Memories of Christmases

past are often the best

Christmas presents.

The
Heart is
Blest

It is in loving, not in being loved,

that the heart is blest;

It is in giving, not in seeking gifts,

that we find our quest.

If you crave the songs of Christmas,

sing out for all to hear;

If you are sad and comfort need,

then dry another's tear.

Whatever your longing, whatever the need,

is just what you must give;

then your soul will fill, and you indeed,

will truly, fully live.

The Christmas spirit lives inside
gifts given throughout the year,
in smiles to a frightened child,
in a friend who lends an ear…

In gentle hugs for those who hurt
and tender words to say.
These make any moment seem
just like a holiday.

I heard the bells on Christmas Day
their old familiar carols play,
And wild and sweet the words repeat
of peace on earth, good will to men.

I tho't how, as the day had come,
the belfries of all Christendom
Had rolled along th' unbroken song
of peace on earth, good will to men

Then peeled the bells more loud and deep.
God is not dead, nor doth He sleep,
The wrong shall fail, the right prevail
with peace on earth, good will to men.

Till ringing, singing, on its way,
the world revolved from night to day
A voice, a chime, chant sublime,
of peace on earth, good will to men.

—H.W. Longfellow

*W*hen sleigh bells ring with
melodies of yuletides long ago,
when country roads are blanketed
with crisp new-fallen snow,
then thoughts of friends and family,
both near and far away,
bring warm, old-fashioned memories
to share on Christmas Day.

The door will stay unlocked tonight,
The hearthfire will stay aglow;
For I seem to hear soft crunching feet
Of angels in the snow.

My heart is open wide tonight,
For stranger, friend, or kin;
I will not bar a single door
Where love might enter in.

I never saw angelic choirs
or beheld a star above a manger,
but I have witnessed Christmas joy
in the eyes, the voice, of a child,
and that is heaven enough for me.

—Taylor Morgan

There is joy in the world
just looking for a way
into our hearts.

The laughing eyes,
The snowy skies
Where love is strong
And all belong,
Hearts that beat true,
Noel, it's you!

Every star in the sky whispers —
we're all part
of the celebration.

There is a kind of magic
that happens every year
when winter winds are blowing
and nights are cold and clear.

It is then you see it happen
in lights upon a tree,
in crimson bows and frosted panes
and gifts "To You, From Me."

Christmas is that magic;
it works its subtle art,
bringing love and wonder
to every waiting heart.

*If I gave you a gift
it would hold all the joy
that you've brought to my life
through the years.*

*I'd wrap it in love
and memories of
our moments—
my life's souvenirs.*

*The bow on the top
I would tie with a wish
for a life graced
from heaven above.*

*Then I'd send it your way
on a cool Christmas Day
so you'd know
that forever you're loved.*

The Way to Christmas

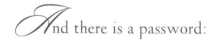

The way to Christmas
is through a little gate,
child-high and child-wide.

And there is a password:
Peace on earth.
May you, this season,
take the hand of a child
and be led
with a new sense
of hope and innocence,
into the world of wonder
that is Christmas.

Christmas is not just a season but a state of mind.
To cherish peace and good will, to be rich in mercy,
and to savor music in one's heart; this is the essence
of the true spirit of Christmas.

If we do these things, a hope will be born within us,
and over us will shine a star,
sending its gleam of hope to all the world.

It is Christmas every time

you let God love others

through you...

every time you smile

at your brother

and offer him your hand.

—*Mother Teresa*

A young Inuit boy listened carefully as a teacher
explained why people give gifts at Christmastime—
to continue the tradition of love and generosity
displayed at the first Christmas.

When December 25 arrived, the boy brought his teacher
a piece of weather-polished whale bone.
"Where did you ever find such a beautiful item?" the teacher asked.

The youth named the spot, several miles away, across the frozen land.
The teacher was touched. "This is beautiful, but you shouldn't have
trekked all that way to get a gift for me."

The boy smiled, eyes shining. "The long walk is part of the gift," he said.

*E*ven better than catching

the Christmas spirit

is allowing the Christmas spirit

to catch you.

Merry is as

Merry Does

*I have always thought of Christmas as a good time:
a kind, forgiving, charitable, pleasant time; the only time
I know of, in the long calendar of the year, when men and women
seem by one consent to open their shut-up hearts freely...*

*And though it has never put a scrap of gold or silver in my
pocket, I believe that it has done me good, and will do me good.*

*And so, as Tiny Tim said, "A merry Christmas to us all;
God bless us, every one!"*

—Charles Dickens